Fight
THE
good
Fight

Fight the Good Fight: Satan's Tactics and Our Defense
Text copyright © 2017 Sovereign Grace Missionary Press

ISBN: 978-0-9983187-2-1 (color), 978-0-9983187-3-8 (b/w)

Scripture quotations from The Authorized (King James) Version. Rights in the Authorized Version in the United Kingdom are vested in the Crown. Reproduced by permission of the Crown's patentee, Cambridge University Press.

Publishing and Design Services: MartinPublishingServices.com

Fight the *good* Fight

SATAN'S TACTICS AND OUR DEFENSE

TREVOR JOHNSON
WITH GRACE RANKIN

Sovereign Grace Missionary Press

Fight

THE

good

Fight

Contents

Introduction

What if you knew you had a prowler around your house? And not just a "harmless burglar" but a mass murderer, someone known for his deception, manic evil intentions, and violence. Someone notorious for having absolutely no mercy, sizing others up for how best to destroy them, and whose mind dwells in the darkest, most satanic places of doom, death, and utter depravity.

You would probably be terrified.

The truth is, we all have a prowler, just not visibly around our homes. His name is Satan: devil, serpent, father of lies, god of this world.

Some Christians downplay his power, rationalizing that since God is in control, we don't have to worry about Satan or even how we should act. As long as we believe in Jesus, everything will be fine.

Others take it too far in the opposite direction, seeing the devil "behind every tree," and even blaming him when they succumb to temptation.

The truth is that Satan is powerful, even terrifyingly so, but he is not sovereign. God is. In this work, we aim to explain from Scripture the extent of Satan's authority and how it relates to God's sovereignty. It is truly frightening to peer into the face of evil like this and realize it is indeed a genuine threat. But it is also comforting to learn of God's absolute control of this world and of our lives. It is heartening to be informed of the complete saving perfection of Christ's work on the cross. And it is emboldening to realize we have a Warrior who promises to fight beside us and provide us with the armor we need to defend ourselves against the blazing arrows of the evil one.

Satan is a real menace, but William Gurnall describes him aptly when he states that our opponent is but "a bungler that hurts and hackles his own legs with his own axe."[1] Even though our foe wages a genuine war against God and His people, every one of his rabid devices ultimately flows only from the wise permission of God, and his venom only contributes to God's glory and the eternal good of the saints—not his own gain. A real spiritual battle rages and Satan lusts to destroy us, but he is so feeble that God uses him as a tool and instrument to greater glorify Himself.

It is our hope that this brief examination of the devil will truthfully present his power in its full terror, unpack the dilemma of God's sovereignty and evil's existence in the world, spread the gospel of Jesus Christ and how His power has already defeated death, and share the tools God has provided us to combat this evil.

Our prayer is that "the peace of God, which passeth all understanding, shall keep your hearts and minds through Christ Jesus"[2] (Philippians 4:7).

---

1 William Gurnall, The Christian in Complete Armour: Or, A Treatise on the Saints' War with the Devil (London: William Tegg, 1862), 69.

2 All Scripture is taken from the Holy Bible, King James Version. (Camden, New Jersey: Thomas Nelson Inc. 1970.)

Fight
THE
good
Fight

1

The Devil Described

Before we examine Satan's deeds, we will paint a general portrait of his character. There are countless features of this biblical antagonist, and we have organized them into four main categories. He is personal, powerful, deceitful, and evil. Scripture illustrates each of these for us in detail.

1. Satan is Personal

Perhaps the most frightening characteristic of Satan is that he is personal. He is not a force and he is not blind. He has a personality and he attacks in particular ways. His nature is twofold—one, he is a unique individual with his own character, choices, decisions, and abilities to reason; and two, he attacks in intimate, specific ways, seeming almost to read people's minds due to his craftiness, and appearing to know their motives due to his understanding of human nature.

There are two aspects of this personal characteristic of Satan. First, he cannot be mistaken for an impersonal force. He exists not merely as a label or a literary device that we place upon earthly misfortune and tragedy. The Bible consistently uses personal pronouns to refer to him. Satan is a real individual. He possesses motivations, plans, and schemes, and he implements them with the deadly cunning of a sentient personality rather than the dumb instincts of an animal.

The different accounts of Satan that we will examine in the next chapter flesh out diverse shades of his dark character until they complete a frightening portrait. The book of Job paints Satan as a schemer. Zechariah depicts him as an accuser in his element. The account of David's sinful census in I Chronicles displays the devil as a cunning opportunist. Together, these three passages show us a highly capable, intimately involved, psychologically learned, and utterly evil personage.

And that leads us to the second aspect of this characteristic, which is that Satan attacks us in personal ways. An impersonal force like the weather may cause tragedy, but Satan is particular and intentional—he knows individuals and how best to seek their demise.

The fury of a tornado is terrifying, but it destroys blindly and targets no one particularly. The devil, however, is brutally perceptive and focuses his hate upon specific Christians. An impersonal force cannot seethe with hatred toward you and plot your destruction, but Satan can and does.

He targets Christians and is their busiest antagonist. Charles Spurgeon warns us, "...as the birds peck most at the ripest fruit, so you may expect Satan to be most busy against you."[3]

As we increase in our Christian life, we might find ourselves more and more the focus of the enemy's evil

---

3 Charles Spurgeon, Satan A Defeated Foe (Springdale, PA: Whitaker House, 1983), 16.

schemes. Spurgeon further points out that few nations war against barren ground or frozen waste but over the most fertile valleys, for "[Satan] wants to pluck God's jewels from His crown."[4]

The devil studies us to know our weaknesses. Charles Spurgeon again instructs us that, "Satan knows how to look at us and size us up from heel to head..." He may pinpoint one man's weakness as lust or sloth or anger and dig his claws into that particular area, ponders Spurgeon, before telling us, "The eye of malice is very quick to perceive a weakness, and the hand of enmity soon takes advantage of it."[5] He continues, "The enemy, like a fisherman, watches his fish, adapts his bait to his prey, and knows in what seasons and times the fish are most likely to bite."[6]

In the book of Job, we see that Satan already knows everything about this righteous man. He asks God, "Doth Job fear God for nought? Hast not thou made an hedge about him, and about his house, and about all that he hath on every side? thou hast blessed the work of his hands, and his substance is increased in the land" (Job 1:9-10). When God asks Satan if he has considered Job, describing him as an upright man who fears God and turns from evil, the answer is yes, Satan has certainly considered Job. He has more than considered him—he knows what Job has and how God has blessed him. This was not a random human being to torment. This was a choice target, a personal vendetta—a chance for Satan to try to turn one of God's own children against Him.

---

4 Ibid, 17.
5 Ibid.
6 Ibid, 27.

Another example from Scripture of Satan's chilling knowledge of particular Christians is found in Luke 22. Jesus tells Peter, "Simon, Simon, behold, Satan hath desired to have you, that he may sift you as wheat: But I have prayed for thee, that thy faith fail not: and when thou art converted, strengthen thy brethren" (Luke 22:31-32). This is an incredible picture: Satan asked permission from God to torment one of His children. He had the gall to make this insidious request of the almighty Creator, who by the way created Satan and the apostle himself. He had to ask Peter's Father if he could *sift him.*

The Blue Letter Bible defines the Greek word *sift* as, "shake in a sieve...try one's faith to the verge of overthrow".[7] The devil *desired* Peter. This word has an intensely negative connotation according to the BLB: "ask for, demand of...in a bad sense...for torture... for punishment".[8] Satan is so thirsty for evil, so bent on destroying the righteous, and so determined to obtain leave to persecute specific children of God that he will go to extraordinary lengths—even requesting permission from the King of kings—for that chance.

What is more, the devil desired *Peter.* His wrath was not merely undirected, but focused upon this one individual. The devil had him in his crosshairs; his sights were laid upon Peter's frame to fell him. His hatred was aimed specifically, and his request was by name.

But just as particularly and just as personally, Christ prayed for Peter. As pointed as Satan's arrows of

---

7 "Sift." Blue Letter Bible. 2016. Accessed Nov. 30, 2016. https://www. blueletterbible.org/lang/lexicon/lexicon.cfm?Strongs=G4617&t=KJV.

8 Ibid, "desire." https://www.blueletterbible.org/lang/lexicon/lexicon. cfm?Strongs=G1809&t=KJV.

destruction were, they disintegrated to nothing under Christ's perfect, personal protection of Peter, which He also reserves for us.

How fortunate Peter was that Jesus Christ Himself— God's own Son—*prayed for him.* For more on Christ's triumphant work, see Chapter 3. For now, we must continue our sketch of the evil one.

2. Satan is Powerful

This personal enemy of ours far surpasses us in ability, intellect, strength, and skill. He is among the "sons of God" in Job and one who masquerades as an "angel of light" according to the Apostle Paul (II Corinthians 11:14). The devil is of such concentrated malevolence that other fallen angels are not his peers but his subordinates, and are actually called "his angels" (Matthew 25:41). He is not merely *among* the fallen angels, but is *head* of their activities and is the *chief antagonist* of God.

This chief antagonist has many alarming abilities:

- He can cause disease ("So went Satan forth from the presence of the LORD, and smote Job with sore boils from the sole of his foot unto his crown" [Job 2:7]. See also Luke 13:16.)

- He can impede the work of evangelism ("Wherefore we would have come unto you, even I Paul, once and again; but Satan hindered us" [I Thessalonians 2:18].)

- He can afflict God's servants ("And lest I [Paul] should be exalted above measure through the abundance of the revelations, there was given to me a thorn in the flesh, the messenger of Satan to buffet me, lest I should be exalted above measure" [II Corinthians 12:7].)

- He can use people as his tools ("And Satan stood up against Israel, and provoked David to number Israel" [I Chronicles 21:1].)

- He can influence some to speak as his mouthpiece ("Then Peter took him [Jesus], and began to rebuke him, saying, Be it far from thee, Lord: this shall not be unto thee. But he [Jesus] turned, and said unto Peter, Get thee behind me, Satan: thou art an offence unto me: for thou savourest not the things that be of God, but those that be of men" [Matthew 16:22-23].)

Satan's power can further be seen in the quickness and ease of the Fall of man. Even in their perfect state, Adam and Eve—with terrifying rapidity and only feeble resistance—succumbed to the frightening power of the devil to destroy all that is good and beautiful.

In fact, with just a question and a declaration—a mere 46 words in English—Satan incited the Fall, setting in motion a deluge of evil that would engulf the world, resulting in the Great Flood, millennia of destruction, and ultimately the death of the Son of God. Of course, this was all according to God's perfect, predetermined plan, and only led to Satan's utter defeat. Even in death, Christ was victorious, rising again from the grave.

The point here, however, is that even though the devil has been fully vanquished, he is by no means weak. His humiliation does not show his impotence. Instead, it displays God's strength. Satan is the deadliest opponent, and only our Savior could have defeated him and his hordes of darkness so completely on the cross, making "a shew of them openly, triumphing over them" (Colossians 2:15).

3. Satan is Deceitful

One of Satan's favorite weapons is deception, evident in Genesis 3 where subtle lies undo Adam and Eve. Notice that Satan does not approach Eve with a ridiculous falsehood, but rather an innocent-sounding question: "Yea, hath God said, Ye shall not eat of every tree of the garden?" (Genesis 3:1) In other words, he smoothly sets a slight shadow of skepticism on her mind; he does not cram an outright lie into it. Eve answers, "We may eat of the fruit of the trees of the garden: But of the fruit of the tree which is in the midst of the garden, God hath said, Ye shall not eat of it, *neither shall ye touch it*, lest ye die" (3:2-3, emphasis added; note she intensifies God's original command).

With Eve's answer—already altered from what God originally stated—Satan sees his opportunity. He wriggles into her brain like the snake he is and makes this bold statement: "Ye shall not surely die" (3:4). Before she can object, he continues, "For God doth know that in the day ye eat thereof, then your eyes shall be opened, and ye shall be as gods, knowing good and evil" (3:5). He combines a question meant to set her off-balance, a statement that completely contradicts what she thought she believed, a half-truth meant to convince her that he knows God like she does, and a promise of power and knowledge—something that appeals to the deepest desires of every human. And with his expert presentation, Eve couldn't refuse.

> And when the woman saw that the tree was good for food, and that it was pleasant to the eyes, and a tree to be desired to make one wise, she took of the fruit thereof, and did eat, and gave also unto her husband with her: and he did eat.

—Genesis 3:6

Satan accomplished his purpose. He deceived the woman. He got inside her head, undermined her beliefs, and appealed to her desire for wisdom and power. She succumbed. And she did more than that: she shared her sin with Adam.

With his lies, Satan killed two birds with one stone. He destroyed two humans with a piece of fruit. He damned humanity with a simple conversation.

His very nature is to lie and beguile (II Corinthians 11:3). He is the father of lies (John 8:44), using half-truths, cunning speech, and even the Word of God—distorted and wrenched out of context—to snare his victims.

Yes, Satan will use Scripture itself in his work. When he tempted Jesus, the deceiver cited passages of Scripture—twisted and misquoted, but Scripture itself. Thankfully, Jesus set the perfect example of how to combat the false use of His word. For more on this weapon against the devil, see Chapter 5.

4. Satan is Evil

His very nature is evil, and this is evident not only in what he does, but in what Scripture calls him. God's word labels Satan with a wide array of epithets to describe him in every dark aspect of his twisted being:

- *Serpent, dragon,* and *deceiver of the whole world* ("And the great dragon was cast out, that old serpent, called the devil, and Satan, which deceiveth the whole world: he was cast out into the earth, and his angels were cast out with him" [Revelation 12:9].)

- *Roaring lion* ("Be sober, be vigilant; because your adversary the devil, as a roaring lion, walketh about, seeking whom he may devour" [1 Peter 5:8].)

- *Wicked one* ("When any one heareth the word of the kingdom, and understandeth it not, then cometh the wicked one, and catcheth away that which was sown in his heart....The field is the world; the good seed are the children of the kingdom; but the tares are the children of the wicked one" [Matthew 13:19, 38].)

- *Murderer* ("Ye are of your father the devil, and the lusts of your father ye will do. He was a murderer from the beginning, and abode not in the truth, because there is no truth in him…." [John 8:44].)

- *Father of lies* ("…When he speaketh a lie, he speaketh of his own: for he is a liar, and the father of it" [John 8:44].)

- *Tempter* ("And when the tempter came to him, he said, If thou be the Son of God, command that these stones be made bread" [Matthew 4:3]; see also I Thessalonians 3:5.)

- *God of this world* and *blinder of the minds of men* ("In whom the god of this world hath blinded the minds of them which believe not, lest the light of the glorious gospel of Christ, who is the image of God, should shine unto them" [II Corinthians 4:4].)

- *Prince of the devils* ("But when the Pharisees heard it, they said, This fellow doth not cast out devils, but by Beelzebub the prince of the devils" [Matthew 12:24].)

- *Prince of the power of the air* ("Wherein in time past ye walked according to the course of this world, according to the prince of the power of the air, the spirit that now worketh in the children of disobedience" [Ephesians 2:2].)

- *Accuser of the brethren* ("…for the accuser of our brethren is cast down, which accused them

before our God day and night" [Revelation
12:10].)

Scripture leaves no doubt as to Satan's character. These
words are serious. They convey an authority and power to
Satan that is not to be ignored. He is a prince, a ruler, and
a god as well as a liar, tempter, accuser, and more.

In addition to identifying Satan with descriptive titles,
the Bible gives him specific names, and these labels have
chilling definitions. The below explanations are taken
from the Blue Letter Bible with Strong's concordance:

- Satan: "superhuman adversary"; "an opponent...
  the arch-enemy of good"[9]

- Beelzebub: "lord of the house...the prince of evil
  spirits"[10]

- Abaddon: "destruction"; "ruin...the name of the
  angel-prince of the infernal regions, the minister
  of death and the author of havoc on the earth";
  "a destroying angel"[11]

- Apollyon: "Destroyer...the angel of the
  bottomless pit"[12]

---

9   Ibid, "Satan." https://www.blueletterbible.org/lang/lexicon/lexicon.
    cfm?Strongs=H7854&t=KJV.
10 Ibid, "Beelzebub." https://www.blueletterbible.org/lang/lexicon/lexicon.
    cfm?Strongs=G954&t=KJV.
11 Ibid, "Abaddon." https://www.blueletterbible.org/lang/lexicon/lexicon.
    cfm?Strongs=G3&t=KJV.
12 Ibid, "Apollyon." https://www.blueletterbible.org/lang/lexicon/lexicon.
    cfm?strongs=G623.

These names, together with the descriptive titles, give us a well-rounded picture of Satan's nature and inform us of exactly whom we are dealing with.

To Sum Up

Satan is vindictively personal. He is frighteningly powerful. He is utterly deceitful. And he is absolutely evil. Chapter 2 explores three Old Testament passages which provide clear examples of his nature in action.

Fight

THE

good

Fight

2

The Devil's Dominion

Zechariah 3, I Chronicles 21, and Job chapters 1 and 2 each emphasize different aspects of the devious character of our foe. Satan is an accuser and adversary, he is a roaring lion who constantly prowls, and he is a tempter and opportunist who snatches up every occasion to work evil. By studying these sketches, we may better know our enemy and avoid his traps.

Zechariah 3 – Satan as Accuser and Adversary

Though other "adversaries" appear in Scripture (I Samuel 29:4; II Samuel 19:22) and even the Angel of the Lord is described as an "adversary" in Numbers 22:22, "the" Adversary—Satan the Accuser—appears in Zechariah 3.

Whereas Jesus is our comforter and advocate in this passage—even in His pre-incarnate state—Satan reveals himself to be the prosecutor who continuously condemns us before the divine tribunal, flagging us as polluted and unclean. Whereas the Holy Spirit convicts us of sin for our good, the Accuser seeks to convict us of sin to our eternal detriment, prodding us with our iniquities to defeat us, make us hopeless, and deflate our boldness in serving God.

> And he [an angel] shewed me [Zechariah] Joshua the high priest standing before the angel of the LORD [Jesus], and Satan standing at his right hand to resist him.

—Zechariah 3:1

The word "resist" or "accuse" here is actually from the Hebrew word "satan", and means "to be or act as an adversary, resist, oppose" and "to attack...accuse".[13]

Satan is chief prosecutor, and most of the time he plies his evil trade without needing outright lies. His accusations sting because they are true, consisting of bare justice without grace, crushing us under their weight. The text here says that even though Joshua was high priest, he was not clean on his own before God: "Now Joshua was clothed with filthy garments, and stood before the angel" (Zechariah 3:3). He needed the righteousness of Christ, and Satan was waiting to take advantage of his unclean state, lurking right beside the Angel of the Lord, ready to accuse Joshua in every way.

Our robes are, indeed, like filthy rags. John MacArthur writes the following about Satan's role as an accuser:

> It is also true that the word "satan" as adversary can also take on a legal meaning. In other words, it could be the word prosecuting attorney, or accuser...He is the one who goes before God and sets indictments before God about His own beloved people. He is the "accuser of the

---

13 Ibid, "Satan." https://www.blueletterbible.org/lang/lexicon/lexicon.cfm?Strongs=H7853&t=KJV.

brethren." He is the prosecutorial attorney who stands at the right hand of God, as it were, indicting us.[14]

This portrait of Satan in Zechariah agrees closely with the depiction of him in Revelation 12:10:

> And I heard a loud voice saying in heaven, Now is come salvation, and strength, and the kingdom of our God, and the power of his Christ: for the accuser of our brethren is cast down, which accused them before our God day and night.

Day and night he accuses us: he is relentless.

Isn't it a strange working of the devil to attack us and wound us concerning our past sins, even while encouraging us to commit new ones? Does it not seem odd that one of his chief means of tormenting believers is to chide us concerning the very evil he promotes?

And yet it is so effective a tactic. I (Trevor) have talked to at least a half-dozen Christians about going into missionary service who ended up never beginning the process of becoming missionaries or, sadly, withdrew from the undertaking when they began to remember and feel the weight of their own past sins. The recollection of such things stole away their boldness and stripped them of holy ambitions. One man, with tears in his eyes, asked me, "How can I even dare to do something like this for God after all I have done?" Another remarked, "I feel like an imposter trying to represent God after my past sins." These former offenses made them cowards, caused them to shrink back from the fight, and stripped them of all

---

14 John MacArthur, "The Character of Satan," sermon preached at Grace Community Church, Panorama City, CA, 2000.

energetic action. The Cross had paid for their sins, and yet these old wounds made them lame for service.

But this is not how the Holy Spirit works. The Holy Spirit may convict us of sin to cause repentance, lead us to holy action, and cleanse us for further more effective service, while the devil's reminders are aimed to sideline us and put us on the bench.

Regarding this point, Spurgeon recalls John Bunyan's *A Pilgrim's Progress*, and writes,

> Bunyan describes Apollyon as standing across the road and swearing by his infernal den that the pilgrim should go no further. There would he spill his soul. Then he began to fling at him all manner of fiery darts. Among them was this one. "Thou didst faint at first setting out, when thou wast almost choked in the gulf of Despond. Thou wast almost persuaded to go back at the sight of the Lions. Thou hast been false already to thy new Lord!"[15]

"Surely God would not and cannot tolerate such a one as you in His holy presence," Satan whispers to our hearts. *"Surely you cannot think you are even the slightest bit holy enough to approach our mighty God or to even dream of inhabiting His holy heaven. Why even try; why not give up this useless charade?"*

But the beautiful thing, dear Christian, is that Satan's never-ceasing business of accusing and opposing the saints to God's face is *shattered* by the cleansing power of grace. We will unpack this amazing truth in Chapter 3.

---

15 Spurgeon, 71.

I Chronicles 21 – Satan as an Opportunist, Tempter, and Inciter

From the account of David's sinful census-taking, we see that Satan is an opportunist without equal. He is not all knowing—he cannot read minds. But Satan can and does read people's characters keenly. A stalking lion (I Peter 5:8), he stealthily lies in wait until his victims slumber, pouncing immediately when opportunities, such as our pride or insecurity, arise.

In I Chronicles 21, we read of Satan stirring up David to number the people, acting as a tempter and inciter of sin. "And Satan stood up against Israel, and provoked David to number Israel" (I Chronicles 21:1). David speaks to his general, Joab, commanding him to carry out this census. At this point, Joab actually tries to dissuade David, asking why he feels the need to do this vain, sinful thing. Pride pollutes David's motives and Satan quickly takes advantage of the situation, fanning these sparks of sin in the king until they produce a deadly conflagration. David does not listen to Joab's counsel, but convinces him to obey his decree.

Here we see an oft-repeated pattern of how God's sovereignty works despite and yet through human sin. All things fulfill His purposes, whether willingly or unwillingly. We sin. In righteous anger, God sometimes chooses to deliver us over to it. Romans 1 describes this occurrence with morbid accuracy: "Wherefore *God also gave them up* to uncleanness"; "For this cause *God gave them up* unto vile affections"; "And even as they did not like to retain God in their knowledge, *God gave them over* to a reprobate mind" (Romans 1:24, 26, 28, emphasis added).

Satan, the opportunist par excellence, then uses this opportunity to further our fall, sow discord, and otherwise cause pain. For the true Christian, however, God grants the grace of repentance, using even sin as a chastening rod for the outworking of His purposes and the good of His children.

The account of David's census illustrates this cycle well. David grows prideful and the devil excites him to greater pride, all of this occurring with God's permission. David rejects his general's warnings and persists in sin *for ten months*. Due to the representative nature of David's position, the nation suffers for his sins until he repents before the Lord. Despite man's sin and the devil's opposition, the Lord accomplishes His will. And despite the fact that David stubbornly persists in rebellion for nearly a year, he still experiences the gracious repentance, forgiveness, and grace of a just and holy yet merciful God.

Job 1 and 2 – Satan as an Opponent of God and Bringer of Misery

There came a day when the sons of God gathered in the Lord's presence, and Satan was there with them. Who were these sons of God? The Psalms and the book of Daniel describe them briefly (Psalm 29:1; 82:1; 89:6-9; Daniel 7:9-10), and phrases such as "angelic congregation," "celestial court," and "heavenly council assembly" spring to mind.

Did these sons of God have regular meetings? We cannot know for sure, but this assembly does not appear to be a mere chance encounter. These sons of God came with the purpose to "present themselves." This presentation was seemingly as a group, a royal summons from the King.

Satan is set apart from this crowd as being a distinctive character. He is among it, an angel, and yet strikingly different from the others present before God's throne. "[T]he sons of God came...and Satan came also."[16] Satan, who may have sung with the sons of God at creation (Job 38:7), is now in the midst of this heavenly assembly seeking to destroy man, the crown of God's handiwork.

When questioned regarding his whereabouts, Satan is purposely vague and deceptive. He was "just roaming about". After all, God questions the devil concerning his assessment of Job, and from his response we see that either he is lying in an effort to provoke God or he is unable to fathom that someone would actually worship God because of who He is and not merely because of what they can gain from Him. Satan brazenly asks, "Doth Job fear God for nought?" (Job 1:9). He is a prosecutor who desires a verdict on human nature and casts doubt concerning Job's motivations in serving God. He is an inciter who questions whether Job's fear of God is even good for anything unless he gets something in return.

When given the opportunity by God, Satan takes every chance he has to destroy Job's life, obliterating all of his earthly wealth and possessions, murdering his servants and children, and turning his own wife against him. To

---

16 John E. Hartley, The Book of Job (Grand Rapids: Eerdmans Publishing, 1988), 72.

top off his works of misery and suffering, Satan strikes Job with painful, horrific boils on every part of his body. There is not a shred of mercy anywhere in the devil.

In fact, it may be that the devil, out of all the inflictions that he could have cast upon Job, studied out that which he calculated would afflict him the most. Spurgeon muses,

> Perhaps the evil one had even inspected Job's personal sensitivities, and so selected that form of bodily affliction which he knew to be the most dreaded by his victim. He brought upon him a disease which Job may have seen and shuddered at, in poor men outside the city gates.[17]

The one thing he does not do is take Job's actual life, and only because God explicitly forbade him from doing so.

This unfathomable cruelty and the troubling realization of how truly evil Satan can be are only assuaged and relieved by the truth of Christ's cleansing, healing, omnipotent, triumphant, victorious power, illustrated in the next chapter.

Satan as Our Worst Enemy

Satan is personal, powerful, deceitful, and evil. He is an accuser, an inciter, and a destroyer. We have seen who he is, and we have seen what he does.

Although God is omnipotent and ultimately in control, the devil still has power. And that isn't the worst of it. There is more bad news.

---

17 Spurgeon, 33.

Even though Satan is called the father of lies, there is one time he is truthful. And that is when he tells God—describes in detail—just how sinful *we* are:

> When God initiates the conversation and asks Satan if he's ever considered **YOU**, Satan reminds him of your lustful thoughts, bad words and improper deeds. He points out your faults and he questions your sincerity. He reminds God of your public sins and your private inappropriate thoughts. Unfortunately, there is no lack of evidence against you. As Satan finishes with glee in his eyes, God glances towards Christ, the Advocate, for a response. Jesus nods and agrees with Satan. It is all true. Everything the accuser has said about you is true. It is the ONLY time that Satan will tell the whole truth—when he is pointing out your sins before a Holy God.[18]

When Satan recounts every disgusting deed we have done, every cruel word we wish we could take back, and every repulsive thought we have indulged before God Himself, he doesn't leave anything out. He tells the entire damning truth. In fact, Revelation 12:10 says that he accuses us before God "day and night".

How are we to stand under such truth? The evidence is stacked against us.

---

18 Rod Arters. Satan's Voice – In the Bible or in Your Head. https://rodarters. wordpress.com/2012/09/04/satans-voice-in-the-bible-or-your-head/.

Fight
THE
good
Fight

BEFORE THE THRONE OF GOD ABOVE

Before the throne of God above
I have a strong and perfect plea;
A great High Priest, whose Name is Love,
Who ever lives and pleads for me.

My name is graven on His hands,
My name is written on His heart;
I know that while with God He stands
No tongue can bid me thence depart.

When Satan tempts me to despair,
And tells me of the guilt within,
Upward I look, and see Him there
Who made an end of all my sin.

Because the sinless Savior died,
My sinful soul is counted free;
For God, the Just, is satisfied
To look on Him and pardon me.

Behold Him there, the risen Lamb!
My perfect, spotless Righteousness,
The great unchangeable I AM,
The King of glory and of grace.

One with Himself, I cannot die;
My soul is purchased by His blood;
My life is hid with Christ on high,
With Christ, my Savior and my God.

—Charitie Lees Smith

3

The Downfall of Death

Things look bleak, hopeless, and frightening...right? They do. But only apart from the most miraculous truth of all: the person and work of Jesus Christ. He is the Light of the world, and when He shines, all darkness flees—even Satan himself.

This is where the good news finally comes in. So how do we stand under the damning truth of the devil? The answer is we don't do anything in our own power, but in the power of Christ. It is *what our Savior has done for us* that will be death's downfall. It is not due to our goodness or worth that we may approach our Holy God. It is entirely because of the goodness of our Lord Jesus Christ.

> And then underneath a radiant white robe, Jesus slowly reveals the scars on His hands. The Savior reminds the heavenly courtroom that all those sins were paid in full—on the cross—for those who trust in Him. Satan slithers away, the case is dismissed and you remain in good standing before God, "*not on the basis of deeds which you have done in righteousness, but according to His great mercy*" (Titus 3:5).[19]

Yes, Satan is cruel. He is powerful. He is evil incarnate.

---

19 Ibid.

But our hope is not in our own strength, nor is it in what we can do. It is in our Savior, the Son of God Incarnate, and what He has already done.

> And I heard a loud voice saying in heaven, Now is come salvation, and strength, and the kingdom of our God, and the power of his Christ: for the accuser of our brethren is cast down, which accused them before our God day and night. And they overcame him by the blood of the Lamb, and by the word of their testimony...

—Revelation 12:10-11

Seeing Job's suffering, David's nearly year-long descent into complete rebellion, Satan's obvious thirst for the death even of a high priest, and the fact that God allowed all of these things is frightening. But we are not doomed to succumb to such oppressive evil during our stay on earth. We are not at the complete mercy of such a cruel foe.

God has not left us on this earth alone. We have the power of the blood of the Lamb. Remember our discussion of Peter? How Christ is our intercessor and His word trumps Satan's every time? Peter's Savior knew what was coming when Satan asked God if he could sift the apostle, and Jesus interceded on Peter's behalf.

How fortunate we are that He intercedes for us in the same way: "For in that he himself hath suffered being tempted, he is able to succor them that are tempted" (Hebrews 2:18); "Wherefore he is able also to save them to the uttermost that come unto God by him, seeing he ever liveth to make intercession for them" (Hebrews 7:25). How blessed we are that Christ's prayers will always triumph over Satan's wily speeches.

Remember also our discussion of Joshua the high priest and his unclean state before God? How Satan relished accusing him before God's holiness? Well, the beautiful thing is that Satan's accusations are crushed by the cleansing power of the blood of Christ. Look at Christ's words in Zechariah 3:4:

> And he answered and spake unto those that stood before him, saying, Take away the filthy garments from him. And unto him he said, *Behold, I have caused thine iniquity to pass from thee, and I will clothe thee with change of raiment*" (emphasis added).

This is the beauty of justification. This is the unfathomability of mercy. This is the glorious yet seeming impossibility of grace. Right in the face of Satan, in front of his very eyes, Jesus Christ declares with perfect certainty and absolute authority that He has caused our iniquity to pass from us, separating it as far as the east is from the west (Psalm 103:12). He has justified us—made us right—before a holy God. There is no doubt of our safety from Satan's clutches. Because of our secure position in Christ, we can stand in His presence and not fall. We can stand before our Lord and be considered clean. We can stand up under the accusations of the devil and emerge victorious through the blood of our Savior.

This is a beautiful truth. But it leads us to real and concerning questions. If God is sovereign, why is the devil so powerful? If God hates sin, why can Satan work so much destruction against His kingdom? If God detests evil, why is Satan allowed to approach Him—is he even still allowed to approach Him?

These questions are the perfect introduction to the next and most important trait of Satan, and one that we have not yet outlined fully: *he is under God's control.*

Satan's devices cannot undo us. All things work together for good for God's children (Romans 8:28). The devil is not sovereign nor is he omnipotent. He cannot do anything but by God's permissive will, and God wills only those things that work for His glory and our good. Satan's power is limited by the power of God.

Fight
THE
good
Fight

4

The Dilemma of Sovereignty and the Existence of Evil

If Satan is powerful, can he do whatever he wants? What about God's sovereignty? Can Satan make someone sin? Did he actually force David to take the census that resulted in the sickness and death of the children of Israel, just as he set out to do? Can he appear before God at any time and ask to torment us, even today?

Let's take a look.

Does Satan Have Access to the Presence of God?

One interesting element in the portrayal of Satan in the Old Testament is that he appears before God. When the sons of God present themselves before Him in Job 1, Satan is among them to work evil. In Zechariah 3, he is standing with the Angel of the Lord. In this divine court scene, he plays the prosecution and thunders his accusations of "Guilty! Guilty! Guilty!"

It is clear that Satan approached the throne of God in the Old Testament. In fact, this activity seems to be a frequent theme. But what about now? Can Satan still approach the presence of God to accuse the saints?

From the first advances of the gospel during His earthly ministry, Jesus announced that He saw Satan falling from heaven like lightning (Luke 10:18). Elsewhere, He depicted His ministry as one that acted to bind the "Strongman" and plunder his goods (Matthew 12:29). At this present time, due to the finished work of Christ, the Church is plundering Satan and redeeming the nations to God. Revelation 12 describes the great Dragon being "cast out," "cast down to earth," and as having "no more place" in heaven following the birth of a man-child who would rule the nations with a rod of iron.

My (Trevor) tentative conclusion is that during the Old Testament, Satan had much more mobility and access to the presence of God than he does now. During Christ's earthly ministry, the "Strongman" was bound and the church is now plundering his goods. He has been thrust out of heaven and can no longer accuse the saints in the presence of God (Revelation 12). Though he is full of wrath, knowing that his time is short, he is still a beaten foe and is in full retreat, all of his stolen territories continuing to shrink as we occupy the land. Soon, he will finally be restricted to the Lake of Fire and no longer be free to roam anywhere at all for all eternity.

Who Actually Incited David to Sin?

Something shocking occurs when comparing the two accounts of David's sinful census. In I Chronicles 21:1 the texts states, "And Satan stood up against Israel, and provoked David to number Israel." However, in II Samuel 24:1 we read, "And again the anger of the LORD was kindled against Israel, and he moved David against them to say, Go, number Israel and Judah." Is Scripture contradicting itself here? Who actually incited David to sin?

Though skeptics and atheists have long abused these verses to purport alleged discrepancies in the Bible, these passages are actually blessed gifts of God that allow us to delve more deeply into His sovereignty and the nature of evil. God frequently punishes transgression by withdrawing His restraint upon a person and turning him over to sin (Romans 1:24). Ironically, the punishment for sin is often more sin. John Haley writes, "He has a punitive purpose in granting this permission. He uses evil to chastise evil."[20] David sinned and thus merited the withdrawal of God's grace upon him, an opportunity the devil took to further spur him to iniquity. Thus, God can be said to incite David's actions by withdrawing His grace, even when David's own sinful heart, aided by Satan's evil schemes, is the principal cause of this offense.

In like manner, we witness the interplay between God and Pharaoh. It is written that God hardened Pharaoh's heart: "And the LORD hardened the heart of Pharaoh" (Exodus 9:12; see also Exodus 4:21; 7:3; 10:1, 20, 27; 11:10; 14:4, 8; Romans 9:14-18). But it is also recorded that Pharaoh hardened his own heart: "But when Pharaoh saw that there was respite, he hardened his heart, and hearkened not unto them" (Exodus 8:15; see also vs. 32; 9:34). To further complicate things, we read that Pharaoh's heart was hardened in the passive form without an agent directly indicated: "And the magicians

---

20 John W. Haley, Alleged Discrepancies of the Bible (Grand Rapids, Michigan: Baker Book House, 1977), 142.

of Egypt did so with their enchantments: and Pharaoh's heart was hardened, neither did he hearken unto them" (Exodus 7:22; see also vs. 14; 8:19; 9:7, 35).

Which of these statements is correct? Well, we know Scripture never contradicts itself. Thus, all statements are true. We can understand this by realizing that Pharaoh was never forced against his will. Rather, God removed His common grace from him and provided the providential circumstances such that Pharaoh was turned over to sin and became increasingly hardened, willingly choosing evil instead of good.

Since the nature of mankind is totally fallen, dead, and depraved, God does no injustice by removing some of His common grace from a sinner. In so doing, He merely allows the transgressor to follow his own evil will; thus, the sinner falls by his own weight. God doesn't force a sinner to sin—sinning is our natural bent, our accustomed way, and our wicked heart's desire apart from His grace.

Consider this analogy of a rabid dog restrained by a chain. Just as the creature strains at his chain to do harm, sinful man strains at God's chain of common grace which prevents him from being as evil as he could possibly be. Mankind is totally depraved, but not always as depraved as he could be in every situation. He is ruined in whole and in every part, and yet does not always maximize his opportunities to do evil due to God's common grace. God restrains even the unsaved and prevents the full extent of their capacity for evil from becoming manifest.

God sometimes chooses to loosen that chain, however, and allow more room to roam. He causes no sin, and yet God does not always restrain every sin but often chooses to withdraw His restraining influence from sinners. They are "turned over" to sin, or, as the language of Romans 1:24, 26, and 28 tells us, God "gave them over" or "gave them up" to their own sinful desires. God does not force them to sin but only allows them to do as they please. Salvation, on the other hand, is God saving us from ourselves and from our own natures, changing our hearts and appetites.

This total depravity of mankind merits damnation. Therefore, God is just and holy when He uses pre-existing evil for His greater purposes and removes His common grace in response to human sin, even if this removal results in more sin. Augustine asserts that the will of God is never evil "because even when it inflicts evil it is just, and what is just is certainly not evil."[21]

Who Afflicted Job?

God is not to blame for our evil ways. But what about suffering that happens to righteous people like Job? In Job's story, it would appear that Satan tormented him, but if the Lord gave the devil permission, isn't it ultimately God's fault?

In Job 1:12, God hands everything Job calls his own—even his precious children—into Satan's dominion: "And the LORD said unto Satan, Behold, all that he hath is in thy power..." And in chapter 2:6, God grants Satan the final authority to hurt Job himself: "And the LORD said unto Satan, Behold, he is in thine hand; but save his life." Scripture then says, "So went Satan forth from the

---

21 Augustine, The Enchiridion of Faith, Hope and Love, translated by Thomas S. Hibbs (Washington, D.C.: Regnery Gateway, 1996), 119.

presence of the LORD, and smote Job with sore boils from the sole of his foot unto his crown" (Job 2:7). When God gives Satan permission to harm Job's belongings, the devil uses bands of Sabean and Chaldean warriors and a great fire to attack Job's servants and animals, and then a great wind from the wilderness to collapse a building on every one of Job's children—all in the same day. And when God allows Satan to hurt Job, Satan personally descends from the presence of the Lord and strikes Job with painful, bulbous lesions. The devil is far from passive in this dark narrative; he is the chief instigator of Job's suffering and anguish.

Yet when Job is afflicted, he answers that it is the Lord who gives and the Lord who takes away (Job 1:21). Scripture asserts that Job "sinned not, nor charged God foolishly" (Job 1:22). When Job receives the report that a great fire has destroyed his sheep and servants, he is told, "The fire of God is fallen from heaven" (Job 1:16). When God grants further power to Satan to afflict Job's body, Job again replies, "What? shall we receive good at the hand of God, and shall we not receive evil?" (Job 2:10). Job appears to credit God with causing all of his distress (Job 42:11), and yet we are told that in all of this Job did not sin.

Whose fault is it? Satan's or God's? Like the above example with Pharaoh, both of these assertions are true. First, we must realize that Satan could do nothing apart from God. Even though he wreaked havoc on every aspect of Job's life, he had to ask permission first. He was not able to act on his own. God in His omniscience knew exactly what Satan would do, when he would do it, and how Job would react. Every second of Job's fiery, painful trial, he was safe in the hand of Almighty God.

The Lord does give, and the Lord does take away. But He sometimes uses Satan as an agent and allows him to test His children. But this leads to the burning question: how can a sovereign God who is good allow so much evil?

God's Use of Evil for His Own Glory

How can an all-powerful God be good if He can end evil yet chooses not to? How can we worship a God who has not only allowed Satan to fall, but has also allowed him to exist as an enemy for multiple ages? How can it be said God does not cause evil while He permits wicked spirits to afflict people?

First, God is acting right now to destroy evil. He is ending wickedness in the world for His glory and His people's ultimate good. We may not understand His ways, but we are promised that "all things work together for good" (Romans 8:28).

Second, although God did permit evil to enter the world, He did not cause it to do so. Now that it has entered, He uses it—as He does everything—"according to the good pleasure of His own will" (Ephesians 1:5, 11) and "to the praise of His glory" (Ephesians 1:12, 14). He allowed evil into the world in order to maximize the display of His divine attributes. After all, mercy is only seen if there is misery, wrath is only exercised in judgment, and forgiveness is only shown in the presence of transgression. Without sin's entrance, the work of

Christ—the highest expression of both love and wrath—would be unneeded.[22]

But *why* does God will evil to happen? To understand this, it is helpful to recognize the two aspects of God's will: His *prescriptive will* and His *decretive will*. His prescriptive will is His will of command—what He desires for mankind and the world, what is revealed to us. We find it disclosed in Scripture.

God's decretive will is His will of decree—what He has decreed will actually happen, His sovereign will, His decree of particular events and happenings, and something we will not understand on this earth. It is His secret will.

But how does this relate to God allowing evil?

We can affirm that even the Fall was within the *decretive will* (or secret decree) of God, for Christ is referred to as the "lamb slain from the foundation of the world" (Revelation 13:8). It was not, however, part of His *prescriptive will* (His revealed desire), as we can see from His punishment of the sin that entered and by His decision to send the Flood.

Before sin's arrival, God had already prepared its atonement. Likewise, we as believers are "chosen in Him from before the foundation of the world" (Ephesians 4:2). God is not the author of sin, but He uses already-existing evil for His own ends (Amos 3:6; Isaiah 45:7). He does not desire sin and evil, but He uses it to magnify His name and accomplish His divine purposes.

---

22 Norman L. Giesler, Philosophy of Religion (Eugene, Oregon: Wipf & Stock Publishers, 2003), 389.

Satan as the Unwitting Instrument of God

This leads us to the point that just as God uses evil to accomplish His purposes, so He uses Satan. William Gurnall illustrates this in the following selection:

> We find Christ was not led of the evil spirit into the wilderness to be tempted, but of the Holy Spirit, Matthew 4:1. Satan tempts not when he will, but when God pleaseth, and the same Holy Spirit which led Christ into the field, led him off with victory. And therefore we find him marching in the power of his Spirit, after he had repulsed Satan, into Galilee, Luke 4:14. When Satan tempts a saint, he is but God's messenger, II Corinthians 12:7. 'There was given to me a thorn in the flesh, the messenger of Satan to buffet me.'...The devil never meant to do Paul such a good office, but God sends him to Paul, as David sent Uriah with letters to Joab; neither knew the contents of their message.[23]

Here we see that the Holy Spirit led Christ to His trial— He led Him to where He would be subjected to every dark and evil temptation Satan could conjure. Hebrews 4:15 says, "For we have not an high priest [Jesus] which cannot be touched with the feeling of our infirmities; but was *in all points tempted like as we are*, yet without sin" (emphasis added). Christ experienced every kind of temptation, and yet He endured these satanic attacks without sin. What was a horrific, painful, and incredibly dark time for Christ only enhanced His perfect example

---

23 William Gurnall, The Christian in Complete Armour: Or, A Treatise on the Saints' War with the devil (London: William Tegg, 1862), 69.

to us, allowing the writer of Hebrews to comfort us with Christ's absolute perfection as our High Priest.

Although Satan tempts us and works evil in the world, he does so as an agent of God's sovereign will. Unknowingly, he does exactly what God wants him to do.

We know from the book of Job that God is ultimately in control. He merely uses Satan to accomplish His own will with Job. Elsewhere in the Bible, God frequently uses demons as instruments of His wrath. He sends an evil spirit to influence Abimelech and the men of Shechem (Judges 9:23ff), a lying spirit to punish King Ahab (I Kings 22:22-23; II Chronicles 18:19-22), and an evil spirit to trouble King Saul (I Samuel 16:14). In Job's case, God uses Satan to afflict His servant, but not for any sin.

God uses *all things* to His own glory. He even deems it appropriate to use the devil himself to accomplish His divine will. John Calvin makes it plain that "Satan is clearly under God's power, and is so ruled by his bidding as to be compelled to render him service."[24] In Job, I Chronicles, and Zechariah, we see Satan striving against God's people, but only succeeding in accomplishing the will of God.

Satan is Completely Under God's Control

Though unwilling, Satan is God's servant and instrument, His devil who reluctantly fulfills His plans. Satan is not

---

24 John Calvin, Institutes of the Christian Religion, Volume I, translated by Henry Beveridge. Edinburgh: Calvin Translation Society, 1854; reprint Grand Rapids: Eerdman's, 1958, Book I: 17.

sovereign, and the war that he wages against God is not an equal match. Satan is not even a contender, "but a rebel to whom God gives as much rope as will glorify His name."[25]

Calvin writes:

> For the disposition of the devil being wicked, he has no inclination whatever to obey the divine will, but, on the contrary, is wholly bent on contumacy and rebellion. This much, therefore, he has of himself, and his own iniquity, that he eagerly, and of set purpose, opposes God, aiming at those things which he deems most contrary to the will of God. But as God holds him bound and fettered by the curb of his power, he executes those things only for which permission has been given him, and thus, however unwilling, obeys his Creator, being forced, whenever he is required, to do Him service.[26]

Even when Satan sends disease and trials to believers, God is behind the scenes, orchestrating all to His own glory such that the devil only does His will. John Piper illustrates this from the Apostle Paul's "thorn in the flesh." Piper writes, "This thorny 'messenger of Satan' was designed by God for sanctifying, gospel purposes well beyond the reach of Satan. Satan becomes the lackey [servant] of the risen Christ."[27] Turretin likewise writes, "The devil is no more than the servant of God, the keeper

---

25 Frederick Leahy, Satan Cast Out: A Study in Biblical Demonology (Carlisle, Pennsylvania: Banner of Truth Trust, 2004), 36.

26 John Calvin, Institutes of the Christian Religion, Volume I, translated by Henry Beveridge. Edinburgh: Calvin Translation Society, 1854; reprint Grand Rapids: Eerdman's, 1958, Book I: 17.

27 John Piper, God Is the Gospel: Meditations on God's Love as the Gift of Himself (Wheaton, Illinois: Crossway Books, 2005), 128.

of the prison, who has no power over sinners unless by the just judgment of God."[28]

Satan Must Ask Permission

Satan had to receive permission from God before harming Job in any way. He "could not even mention Job until God invites him to do so."[29] God begins the conversation and names Job. It may appear that Satan provokes God into a wager at Job's expense, and yet it is God who orchestrates events. Rather, God summons Satan in front of all and brings the name of Job up before the gathered assembly. God is the initiator, and "the main function of this assembly here is to provide an open forum in which Yahweh permits the testing of Job."[30]

Satan is the active—yet ultimately powerless—dupe. He is merely used by God to teach the world a lesson about suffering through Job. It is significant that Job is chronologically the first book in the Bible. The most ancient scroll in Scripture meets one of the oldest questions of philosophy: "Why is there pain and suffering?" The lessons of Job are enduring, relevant even to 21st century man, for he still suffers and needs the comfort of knowing that Satan can do nothing more than he is permitted. Definite bounds are set to his activities. What Satan meant for evil God still uses for good thousands of years

---

28 Francis Turretin, "On The Necessity of the Atonement," translated by James R. Wilson in James R. Wilson, A Historical Sketch of Opinions on the Atonement. Philadelphia, Pennsylvania: James Earle, 1817, 224.

29 H.L. Ellison, From Tragedy to Triumph (Carlisle, Pennsylvania: The Paternoster Press, 1958), 25.

30 Hartley, 72.

later (see Genesis 45:5, 50:20). Christians today continue to turn to Job's trial for encouragement, comfort, and answers to face their own hardships and distresses.

Because of Job's afflictions, we now have a book of great comfort, as Spurgeon writes: "The devil went to the forge and worked away with all his might to make Job illustrious! Foolish devil! He was piling up a pedestal on which God would set his servant Job, that he may be looked upon with wonder by all ages." He concludes, "If you want to make the devil angry, throw the story of Job in his face."[31]

By the end of the book of Job, it is God who is the main character. Satan "fills a subservient role" and "is cast off as of no further interest, and is not even mentioned at the close of the story."[32] John Calvin writes:

> With regard to the strife and war which Satan is said to wage with God, it must be understood with this qualification, that Satan cannot possibly do anything against the will and consent of God. For we read in the history of Job, that Satan appears in the presence of God to receive his commands, and dares not proceed to execute any enterprise until he is authorized.[33]

Reminiscent of Job's trial, Jesus tells Peter that Satan desired, i.e., requested permission, to sift him like wheat. Also reminiscent of Job is that even these trials serve God's good purposes. *Jesus did not eliminate the trial but prayed that Peter's faith would not fail* and that, when turned, Peter would strengthen the others (Luke 22:31).

---

31 Spurgeon, 39.
32 Leahy, 36.
33 Calvin, Book I, section 17.

Jesus assured Peter that victory was certain and would even lead to others being strengthened, though Peter was not spared the sifting.

Where did this petition take place? Did Satan ask Christ Himself? Although we don't know, I (Trevor) find this probable. If Satan made this request to God in heaven, then we may have another instance of the devil approaching the throne of God, a conclusion that creates tension with my earlier assertion that his access to the throne has been severely restricted by the work of Christ. However, this request would have occurred before the defeat of Satan at the Crucifixion, and so is still a possibility.

Whatever one's opinion regarding the location of this petition, this satanic request is another frightening and shocking evidence that the devil knows us and may ask for us by name. Satan desired to sift Peter until nothing was left, but God allowed this sifting to remove the chaff from Peter so that when he had recovered he would be a source of strength to others.

If Satan must ask permission from God to sift Peter and torment Job, why would God allow such a thing in the first place? Why wouldn't God's response always be a firm no? *"No Satan! You may not sift Peter!"* John Piper answers as follows:

> It's clear from the whole N.T. that God intends to bring the bride of Christ to perfection through affliction and temptation (1 Peter 1:6; 3:17). We must suffer with Christ if we would be glorified with him (Romans 8:17). Through suffering and trial our faith is refined. We are drawn to rely ever more heavily on God and we are moved to cherish his grace more strongly. Satan has his

role to play in fanning the flames of our refining furnace and so God awaits the appointed day of judgment.[34]

In Philippians 1, we see that it is actually a privilege to suffer for Christ's sake: "For unto you it is given in the behalf of Christ, not only to believe on him, but also to suffer for his sake" (Philippians 1:29). In Proverbs, we are told that when we suffer and are disciplined, it is because we are loved: "My son, despise not the chastening of the LORD; neither be weary of his correction: For whom the LORD loveth he correcteth; even as a father the son in whom he delighteth" (Proverbs 3:11-12). To suffer is an honor. It shows how greatly we are loved, with what detail God is attentive to our lives, and how much He delights to care for our spiritual enrichment and fulfillment.

Satan's Power is Not Absolute, But Neither is It Trifling

Theologian Gregory Boyd and others have reacted against "Calvinistic theodicies". A theodicy is a theological or philosophical explanation of why evil endures despite God's existence. It is a defense of God's goodness despite the actuality of evil.

Boyd argues against these Calvinistic defenses by charging that such theodicies discount the reality of the warfare that is taking place. He asserts in his book *God At War* that, "If all evil is believed to serve a higher divine purpose, then clearly one's sense of urgency in fighting it

---

34 John Piper, "The Sifting of Peter," sermon preached on April 26, 1981, Bethlehem Baptist Church, Minneapolis, MN.

is compromised."[35] In other words, if all evil is meant for good, what use is there for us to fight against it?

Boyd elsewhere states, "If Satan's activity is part of God's plan, how can it be said that Satan is God's enemy?" [36] This, however, is faulty logic and leads to this erroneous conclusion: if Satan is not an enemy of God because he performs God's will, then we must not be enemies of God because we perform His will. This simply is not true. The Bible says, "whosoever therefore will be a friend of the world is the enemy of God" (James 4:4).

But Boyd maintains that to stress God's absolute control and even His use of the devil as an instrument is to belittle the deadly ferocity of this warfare. This is also false reasoning. Bible scholar Clinton Arnold warns us, "While Satan's authority is not absolute, neither is it trifling. He wields all kinds of destructive influence over all levels of life and exerts his greatest hostility against God's redemptive purpose in and through the Lord Jesus Christ."[37]

John Calvin affirms the sharp fangs of the devil when he draws this frightening picture: "An enemy relentlessly threatens us, an enemy who is the very embodiment of rash boldness, of military prowess, of crafty wiles, of untiring zeal and haste, of every conceivable weapon and of skill in the science of warfare."[38] Though he can do nothing without permission, once God grants the devil leave to do harm, Satan is an effective and merciless agent. After receiving consent, he afflicted Job with boils

---

35 Gregory Boyd, God at War: The Bible & Spiritual Conflict (Downer's Grove, Illinois: IVP Academic, 1997), 21.

36 Ibid, 201.

37 Arnold, 93.

38 Calvin, Book I, 14, 13.

(Job 2:7), killed his flocks and servants with a storm, and crushed his family with a wind. Satan used these natural disasters, ultimately from the permissive hand of God, to afflict many with misery. Joseph Caryl, a theologian from the 1600s, writes, "The Lord who holdeth the wind in His fists gave Satan power, and he brought a terrible wind."[39] Caryl continues, "When we consider the power and policy of Satan, let us bless God that he cannot stir to do us that mischief which his nature at once inclines and enables him to do, until God permits him."[40]

Satan, that roaring lion, seeks anyone to devour, but he can only devour those for whom he has been given permission. If there was ever a foe to fear, Satan is that foe, and yet God thwarts all of his plans not only by directly opposing him but also by even allowing him a measure of success.

In fact, *take comfort* that the devil is raging upon the earth, for the Scripture says that he does so because his time is short. Revelation 12:12b says, "Woe to the inhabiters of the earth and of the sea! For the devil is come down unto you, having great wrath, because he knoweth that he hath but a short time." His wrath is great because his chances are limited: "We may take it as an assured fact that when he rages to the uttermost, his opportunities are nearly over."[41] The last struggles of a dying animal may be the most dangerous, and a snake may strike out with the most hatred after it has received a mortal wound, but the end is soon.

---

39 Joseph Caryl, Exposition of Job (Lafayette, Indiana: Sovereign Grace Publishers, 1959), 6.

40 Ibid.

41 Spurgeon, 50.

Jesus tells His saints, "I must work the works of him who sent me, while it is day: the night cometh, when no man can work" (John 9:4). The devil, too, has his own sense of urgency, yet uses it to work evil. But his night, too, is coming, a black night which shall never end. Take comfort, dear Christian, that his attacks are but a sign of his desperation, and they will soon cease."

Fight

THE

good

Fight

5

The Duty of Believers

This investigation of Satan in the Old Testament is not merely ivory tower theology—impractical head knowledge we will never actually use. It is immensely relevant and applicable to our daily lives. The three Old Testament passages we examined are case studies of the enemy's strategy, blueprints of Satan's methods of attack.

We know we are safe in the arms of God and that someday we will join Him in glory, but until then, what are we to do? We still live in a world of evil and are still faced with Satan's fiery darts every day (Ephesians 6).

Thankfully, God has given us instructions. We are not to be passive in our avoidance of evil. We are to aggressively combat the devil's attacks. We must (1) prepare our minds, (2) plan to suffer, (3) put on the armor of God, (4) pray, and (5) position ourselves firmly. We must fight the good fight.

1. Prepare Your Mind

Trust in God's Goodness and Sovereignty

The devil loves to attack God's character and His word. Just like the serpent in Genesis 3, Satan slithers into our minds and whispers, "Yea, hath God said?" We must counter with the firm resolve of Job, "Though he slay me, yet will I trust him" (Job 13:15). We must rely upon God who can raise the dead (II Corinthians 1:9), remembering that if we suffer it is only "for our comfort and salvation" (II Corinthians 1:6). Though all things are not good, they work for good for those who love God and who are the called according to His purpose (Romans 8:28). Not even death can separate us from that love of God (vss. 38-39). Even in the worst of cases, momentary earthly misery always precedes eternal heavenly comfort for the saint.

Have confidence that God uses the devil's efforts for our own good. Spurgeon reminds us that, "the temptations of Satan are of a service to the people of God."[42] A guard at night will not slumber if he constantly hears the horrible sounds of the enemy. And Spurgeon beautifully reminds us that, "Children do not run away from their father's side when big dogs bark at them."[43] Praise God for these threats, which cause us to hug our Heavenly Father all the tighter, trust in His strength, and recognize our weakness.

Even when we are totally broken, we are victorious in Christ. Even in death we are not separated from the love of God, and emerge as "more than conquerors through Him that loved us" (Romans 8:37). This extended quote by Charles Spurgeon is worthy to be repeated here for our encouragement:

> The devil must have felt himself small that day when he tried to overthrow Job, dragged him down to a dung hill, robbed him of everything, covered him with sores, and yet could not make him yield. Job conquered when he

---

42 Ibid, 23.
43 Ibid, 24.

cried, "Though He slay me, yet will I trust Him." (Job 13:15). A feeble man had vanquished a devil who could raise the wind and blow down a house, and destroy the family who were feasting in it. Devil as he is, and crowned prince of the power of the air, yet the poor bereaved patriarch sitting on the dung hill covered with sores, being of the woman's seed, through the strength of the inner life won the victory over him.[44]

We are to hold confidently to the fact that God sometimes allows the devil to fan the flames, but He turns this into a refiner's furnace. We are to rest assured in God's providence and trust in His goodness.

Affirm Our Status in Christ

We are children of God; our filth has been removed. The Accuser loves to bring our sins ever before our eyes and defeat us by them. Just as he accused the high priest Joshua and pointed out his genuine uncleanness (Zechariah 3), Satan showcases our sins as evidence that we are unfit to serve God. Thank the Lord that Satan's charges against His people are answered by Jehovah Himself.[45]

As we wage spiritual warfare, we should remember that we are God's children, our sins are forgiven, and past forgiven sins should not defeat us from future useful service. We are saved for service, and Christ's freedom from bondage is a freedom to serve.

Spurgeon tells us to give no heed to the devil's accusations: "Who is he that he should bring an

---

44 Ibid, 141.
45 Leahy, 36.

accusation against us? Let him mind himself. He has enough to answer for. When he turns to being an accuser, it is enough to make the child of God laugh him to scorn." Though Spurgeon does admit that, "Yet it is not easy to laugh when you are in this predicament, for the heart is ready to break with anguish."[46]

We must not let our past sins still our future holy ambitions! Even if we have been great sinners, we should imitate the Apostle Paul, who was the *chief of sinners* and yet the most active of saints. One who conspired to murder, and yet was used by God as a missionary and writer of parts of His Holy Scripture.

Don't Diagnose Every Evil

Not every calamity is because we have a lesson to learn. We need not try to match up particular failures on our part with evils that befall us in a sort of cosmic arithmetic. We are not to be like the disciples who asked about the man born blind, "Who sinned, him or his parents, that he was born blind?" (John 9:2). We are not to assume that those who suffer more are paying for more sins (Job 4:7; 22:5, 23; Luke 13:2-4), but should use these occasions to repent all the more and to thank God for His mercies.

We know that all things work for God's glory and our good even though we cannot list reasons in this life for each evil that overtakes us or our fellow believers. Job was upright, and yet evil descended on his house.

Gregory Boyd, in his book, *Is God to Blame*, opens with an example of a mother losing her baby. This mother

---

46 Spurgeon, 71.

concluded that God took her infant because she was "not ready for children yet," that God "had a lesson to teach her."[47] Boyd is rightly troubled by this conclusion. We are not in the position to make such diagnoses or confidently act as if we know God's purposes. Such foolish proclamations do not bring Him glory.

It is best to leave such conclusions to God alone. He is omniscient, wise, and good, and we must trust in His perfection in times of confusion and tragedy. We should never presume on the will of God, but simply mourn with those who mourn on such sad occasions.

Have Confidence in God Alone

"Finally, my brethren, be strong in the Lord, and in the power of his might" (Ephesians 6:10). Before we put on the armor of God, we must remember that our confidence is not in our own might or abilities, but in God alone.

Charles Spurgeon reminds us that the temptations of the devil act as a "file which rubs off much of the rust of self-confidence."[48] Believers who are lifted up in pride have farther to fall when the devil attacks. In I Timothy 3:6, Paul instructs Timothy not to select leaders who are novices lest they be lifted up and dashed on spiritual rocks by the devil.

A life of humility helps to resist Satan: "Submit yourselves therefore to God. Resist the devil, and he will flee from you" (James 4:6-7). Before we can resist, we are

---

47 Gregory A. Boyd, Is God to Blame?: Moving Beyond Pat Answers to the Problem of Evil (InterVarsity Press, 2003), 11-15.

48 Charles Spurgeon, "Satan Considering the Saints," Metropolitan Tabernacle Pulpit, Volume 11 (Pilgrim Press, 1989), 193-205.

to submit. It is through God's work and His continued power in our lives that we can withstand Satan's attacks.

2. Plan to Suffer

This leads us to our next point: plan to suffer. Note well that our warfare is not one which will spare us from distress (Philippians 1:29).

In his classic, *The Christian in Complete Armour*, William Gurnall states this truth succinctly in the following paragraph about the weapons of our warfare:

> As most of the pieces are defensive, so all of them to defend from sin, none to secure the Christian from suffering. They are to defend him in suffering, not privilege him from it. He must prepare the more for suffering, because he is so well furnished with armor to bear it. Armor is not given for men to wear by the fireside at home, but in the field. How shall the maker be praised if the metal of his arms be not known? And where shall it be put to the proof, but amidst swords and bullets?[49]

Know that even the victorious will suffer much, just as those most vigorous in war may bear the most wounds despite conquering all before them.

Thus, be prepared to fight. Be prepared to suffer in this world. We must arm ourselves for battle!

---

49 William Gurnall, The Christian in Complete Armour, Book II (Banner of Truth Trust, Edinburgh, 1989), 125.

3. Put on the Armor of God

Ephesians 6 perfectly outlines how we are to combat the devil. We are to vigorously resist him. We are to stand firm and fight the good fight. These are active words, not passive ones. We are to be warriors, and we are to exert ourselves to rout evil from our hearts and minds and from the world as we are able. To help us do so, God gives us armor:

> Put on the whole armour of God, that ye may be able to stand against the wiles of the devil. For we wrestle not against flesh and blood, but against principalities, against powers, against the rulers of the darkness of this world, against spiritual wickedness in high places. Wherefore take unto you the whole armour of God, that ye may be able to withstand in the evil day, and having done all, to stand.
>
> — *Ephesians 6:11-13*

Belt of Truth

*Stand therefore, having your loins
girt about with truth.*

—Ephesians 6:14

Being jailed and even bound to Roman soldiers, the Apostle Paul became quite familiar with their attire and weapons. It is no wonder then that he calls upon these martial images as visual teaching tools when he instructs believers how to battle the devil—images that convey the militaristic manner of our fight across all eras, nations, and battles, and that remain relevant today.

The first item he speaks of is a belt. He is thinking of a Roman soldier's belt, that strong leather band his sword sheath was attached to and which kept his tunic in order, allowing him to move about and charge without being hindered. A soldier cannot be ready for battle without such an item, after all.

This is a belt of *truth*. We must know what we believe. We must know the truth that lies in God's word—not a twisted version, but what the Bible truly teaches. Often we don't know what we don't know until we are tested. Therefore, we must not let ourselves be surprised.

The gospel of Jesus Christ, the way of salvation, the role of baptism, and the meaning of communion are just a few of the crucial beliefs Christians must be certain of. Study the Word of God diligently. Analyze the wise works of the early church fathers. Be familiar with their beliefs and logic. But above all, be like the noble Bereans, who "...received the word with all readiness of mind, and searched the scriptures daily, whether those things were so" (Acts 17:11). We are to compare everything we find with Scripture itself.

We must not merely be sure of our beliefs, but we must also be ready to defend the hope we have: "But sanctify the Lord God in your hearts: and be ready always to give an answer to every man that asketh you a reason of the hope that is in you with meekness and fear" (I Peter 3:15).

Furthermore, we must remember that Jesus Christ is "the way, the truth, and the life" (John 14:6). Be grounded in Him. He is the foundation of everything in our lives.

Breastplate of Righteousness

*...and having on the
breastplate of righteousness.*

—*Ephesians 6:14*

Resisting the devil so that he will flee is not a matter of formulaic prayers or methodology; it is a matter of praying and obeying God in a holy life (James 4). It is not passive but active. Satan is hurling fiery darts and temptations at us and we must be ready to withstand them with strength and confidence.

As Dr. Chuck Lawless explains, "Spiritual warfare isn't about naming demons; it's about so living a righteous life that our very life threatens the Enemy."[50] As followers of Christ, we can't just talk the talk. We have to walk the walk.

In his 1828 dictionary, Noah Webster defines righteousness this way:

"Purity of heart and rectitude of life; conformity of heart and life to the divine law...nearly equivalent to holiness, comprehending holy principles and affections of the heart...It includes all we call justice, honesty and virtue, with holy affections; in short, it is true religion."[51]

Christians must act like Christians. To be righteous, we can't merely discuss doctrine or show up at church on Sunday. We should appear radically different from the

50 Chuck Lawless, Disciple Warriors: Growing Healthy Churches That Are Equipped For Spiritual Warfare (Grand Rapids, Michigan: Kregel Publications, 2002), 214.

51 Noah Webster's American Dictionary of the English Language, "Righteousness".

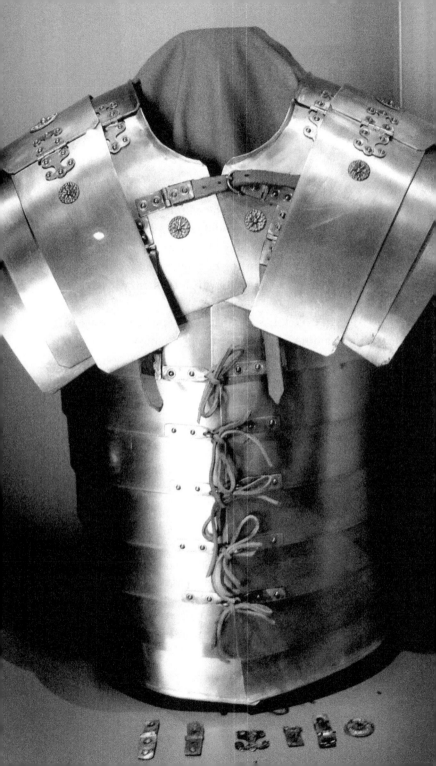

world. We shouldn't blend in. Our speech, actions, and thoughts—our heart, soul, mind, and strength—should point people to Christ. If we look just like the world, why would anyone come to us for the hope we have to offer? We must stand out in righteousness and holy living. Only then will our lights shine and only then will others take note and either hate us or want what we have.

Being righteous involves repenting of our sin. This is a recurrent humility and submission, a turning from our wickedness and conforming to God's standards through His strength and grace. We cannot call ourselves children of God while dwelling in sin of any kind. Although we will never be sinless on this earth, we cannot justify or tolerate the continuance of particular sins in our lives. We must route them, resist them, and run to Christ, begging Him to help us overcome them.

We see that David repented following his sinful census, and in the New Testament, after Peter was sifted and then repented, he did in fact strengthen the brethren (Luke 22:31-34).

We must not give Satan's fiery darts a foothold of any kind. Our vital organs—our hearts—must be protected as if by armor. Such a spiritual breastplate must guard the Christian lest these burning missiles sink deep within and cause mortal wounds. We must resist. We must wear Christ's righteousness in all its purity and not taint it with continuing, unrepentant sin. We do not want our breastplates to rust.

Shoes of the Gospel of Peace

And your feet shod with the
preparation of the gospel of peace.

—*Ephesians 6:15*

The shoes of a Roman soldier were not worn for fashion but for long marches, for pushing against the enemy, and for digging in when the going got tough. Having sure footing is essential because falling in the midst of battle can be fatal.

This armor for our feet consists of the shoes of the gospel. We must know it forward and backward, for it is the most important, the most crucial, and the most meaningful doctrine believers can know.

The gospel is for Christians. It is easy to forget this. It is easy to think, *"Well, now I'm saved. I've heard the gospel. It is for unbelievers, to lead them to Christ."* Although we are to share the gospel with those still in darkness, the good news is first for the children of God. It is easy for us to grow used to the thought—to normalize the message in our minds such that we forget how wonderful it actually is—that Jesus came to earth, died on the cross, and rose again, allowing us to spend eternity with Him when we die.

But *think* about it. *Dwell* on it. Fasten on the shoes of the gospel of peace and don't remove them. Let the gospel overcome and overwhelm your thoughts. Let it overflow in your speech and your life. Let it be such a crucial part of your nature that it comes from you naturally and beautifully—it shines from you like a light on a hilltop (Matthew 5:14-16).

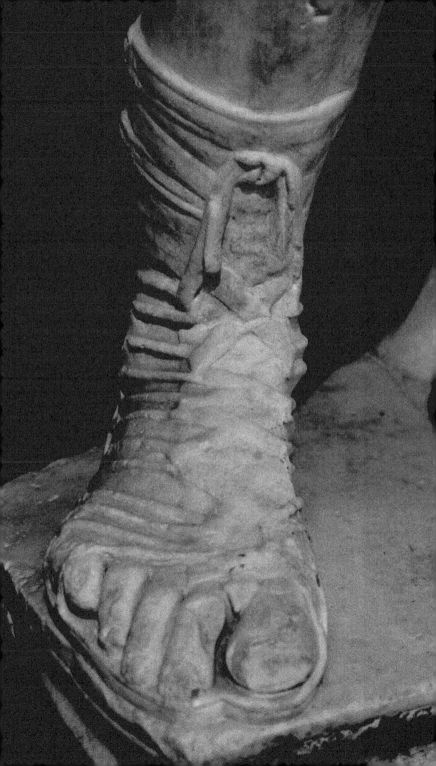

Jesus Christ, the glorious Son of the Almighty God, departed heaven—left His Father who He loved—and lived on earth with sinful, hateful, undeserving men. He was subjected not only to the hunger, thirst, sickness, suffering, and death of this imperfect world, but also to the utter disrespect and cruel treatment of the human beings He created. He was perfectly humble, sinless, and loving, and yet He was rejected, ignored, challenged, hated, used, questioned, chased, betrayed, denied, beaten, tortured, and killed. For us. For depraved, hateful humankind with our black, dead, rebellious, vicious, stony hearts.

But then He was raised. Because Christ's sacrifice was fully perfect, perfectly flawless, and flawlessly whole, God the Father was satisfied. He raised His Son from the dead. Christ's life is the promising seal of our eternal security. Due to His great love, we are pardoned and treasured.

Soak yourself in this beautiful gospel message. Saturate your soul with its glorious truths. It is only when the gospel of Jesus Christ is the foundation of our lives that everything makes sense. The deeper our understanding of Christ's perfect atoning work, the more the things of this earth will grow dim, and we will flourish in the light of His glory and grace, as the beloved hymn "Turn Your Eyes Upon Jesus" describes. The more we understand our beautiful Savior and His beautiful love, the more the words of Paul in Philippians 1 will make sense: "to live *is* Christ and to die is gain" (Philippians 1:21, emphasis added).

Truly, the more we try to wrap our minds around the glory of the Savior we love, the less important the suffering and hardships of this world will be. The more we fill our minds with Him, the less they will be filled with ourselves. The more He occupies our thoughts, the purer our minds will be and the more joyfully our hearts will sing.

Shield of Faith

Above all, taking the shield of faith,
wherewith ye shall be able to quench all the
fiery darts of the wicked.

—Ephesians 6:16

This is the only piece of armor that has a particular attack directly mentioned in regard to it. We are to use our faith to "quench all the fiery darts of the wicked".

Faith is a hugely fundamental, vastly vital foundation of our Christian lives. Faith is that bridge which links us to Christ.

The Blue Letter Bible defines the Greek word used here as:

The conviction that God exists and is the creator and ruler of all things, the provider and bestower of eternal salvation through Christ...a strong and welcome conviction or belief that Jesus is the Messiah, through whom we obtain eternal salvation in the kingdom of God...belief with the predominate idea of trust (or confidence) whether in God or in Christ, springing from faith in the same...[52]

---

52 Blue Letter Bible, "Faith" https://www.blueletterbible.org/lang/lexicon/lexicon.cfm?Strongs=G4102&t=KJV.

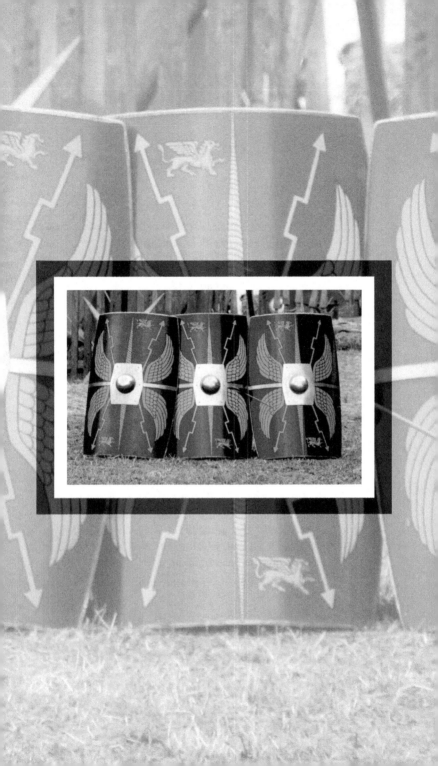

Faith is crucial. We are justified by faith (Romans 5:1), sanctified by faith (Acts 26:18), and saved through faith (Ephesians 2:8). We are to walk by faith (II Corinthians 5:7), live by faith (Galatians 2:20), have joy in the faith (Philippians 1:25), have stability of faith (Colossians 2:5), be sound in the faith (Titus 1:13), and show all good faith (Titus 2:10). Christ Himself is "the author and finisher of our faith" (Hebrews 12:2).

Helmet of Salvation

And take the helmet of salvation.

—Ephesians 6:17

A blow to a peripheral part of the body may cause a limp or a scar, but a wound to the head in battle is often fatal. Every Roman soldier knew that the head is the most vulnerable area and that a strong helmet was essential to his life. Making sure one's head is covered is crucial, thus the Apostle Paul tells us, "Examine yourselves, whether ye be in the faith" (II Corinthians 13:5). Are you wearing this helmet or not?

Peter commands us in his second epistle to "give diligence to make your calling and election sure: for if ye do these things, ye shall never fall" (II Peter 1:10). John Piper reminds us, "The only thing that will fit down the lion's throat is an unbeliever."[53]

We need to make certain we are inedible. Seeing the personality of Satan in its full fury through these three

---

53 John Piper, "The Sifting of Simon Peter (Luke 22;31-34)," sermon preached at Bethlehem Baptist Church, Minneapolis, Minnesota, April 26, 1981.

Old Testament texts, the best defense is to ensure that we are God's children. The slogan, "Smile, God has a wonderful plan for your life," only applies to those who are saved. Uninterrupted physical comfort in this present life is never promised to believers, yet we know that our momentary light afflictions here on earth work for us a far more exceeding and eternal weight of glory (II Corinthians 4:17).

Giving diligence to make one's calling and election sure certainly cuts against the grain of much modern evangelism. I (Trevor) once heard a Baptist pastor give an altar call at a small country church. Uttering a long prayer accompanied by the soft playing of the piano, he summoned people forward to "receive salvation", and then prayed with those who made the journey out of their seats and to the front of the church. Those who came forward were asked to recite a prayer. I was shocked to hear the preacher pronounce at the end of this prayer, *"You are now saved."* Even more alarming was how he followed up this assertion, for he commanded, *"Never doubt it."* On another occasion, I witnessed a similar altar call where the preacher further stated, *"...in the future when you doubt your salvation, remember back to this day, and to what you have done."*

This is foolish presumption! In addition to Paul and Peter's warnings (II Corinthians 13:5; II Peter 1:10), the New Testament does not end before that most excellent small letter of I John, which repeatedly tells us the marks of those who truly believe and those who do not. I John gives us such tests to ask ourselves whether we are keeping His commandments (I John 2:3), whether we are making a practice of sinning (I John 3:4), whether or not we love

others (I John 2:9-10), and whether or not we believe that Jesus is the Christ (I John 5:1). It signifies no lack of faith to test ourselves against these Scriptures.

Know that salvation will change our desires and our thought life. One key test you can do is to ask yourself what you truly desire. If you do not know this, then ask yourself what you always think about. Those things that occupy your mind are what you most desire, for the mind often follows the heart in its course, and much of this may be sin.

The preacher Paul Washer once said in a sermon,

> A lot of people think that Christianity is you doing all the righteous things you hate and avoiding all the wicked things you love in order to go to heaven. No! That's a lost man with religion. A Christian is a person whose heart has been changed; they have new affections.[54]

Check your desires.

Another key test is the question posed in the New Testament: "What think ye of Christ?" (Matthew 22:42). Do you believe in the Jesus portrayed in Scripture? Who is Jesus to you? What does loving Jesus Christ mean to you? What part does He play in your life?

There are some who desire heaven for the joys of heaven. They desire their pain removed. They desire to be safe from any threat of punishment. The streets of gold sound good to them. But they speak nothing of Christ, the center of heaven. Jesus is only an afterthought. If they could have heaven with or without Christ, they would not care. This shows that they do not love God truly above

---

54 Paul Washer, "Dating, Courtship, and Marriage," sermon,
   http://bringingtruth.com/OtherStuff/PaulWasherQuotes.aspx.

all else. What they love is themselves, and they seek their own comfort. They merely use Christ as a means to an end instead of Him being everything to them.

But a saved soul will love the Lord Jesus as He is portrayed in the Scriptures, and will love Him supremely above all else, even his own life.

Sword of the Spirit

...and the sword of the spirit,
which is the word of God.

—Ephesians 6:17

Some commentators have stated that this sword of the Spirit differs from all the other weapons in Paul's list of the full armor of God in that it is an *offensive* weapon rather than a *defensive* one. This may be an oversimplification.

Ephesians 6:17 references the Roman short-sword, the *machaira*, and not the longer *rhomphaia*. This short sword was about 18 inches to two feet long and was used for close-quarter combat, often in the most desperate of fights once the enemy closed with the Roman line of soldiers. Thus, it had both offensive *and* defensive uses.

While a spear may often miss the enemy at a distance, a weapon used at close quarters like the short-sword was sure to draw blood and not come away without effect, whether used defensively or in the attack. Likewise, the Word of God is effective, whether in engaging an unbeliever or answering an objection to the faith. In Hebrews 4:12, we read that it is indeed sharper than a two-edged sword.

Not only is the Word of God sharper than a two-edged sword, but it also never returns void (Isaiah 55:11). I (Grace) had several conversations with someone who held opinions regarding the gospel and salvation that did not add up with Scripture. This is quite dangerous, since the gospel is something we cannot afford to be wrong about! This friend was intelligent and used circular reasoning to confuse the conversations and throw me off track. There were moments I had absolutely no answer except to quote Scripture alone. I felt the debates were not resolved, but as believers, we can trust that God's word never returns void and can rest in the fact that He will do the work.

In the Garden of Eden, Satan sowed seeds of doubt by asking, "Hath God said?" This strategy—questioning God's word—can also be seen during Christ's temptation in the wilderness. But Jesus answered each enticement with the Word of God, using a specific passage to fit the occasion—much like the quick, pointed, carefully-placed stabs of a short-sword. We are to do the same. We are to hold fast to Scripture, storing it away in our hearts for quick access in times of need. We are to cling to it as our solid foundation of truth.

As long as we humbly use Scripture in its proper context to back up our beliefs (and humility is key; no one wants to listen to a haughty, bull-dozer-like defense), we don't have to worry about sounding inadequate or that we have to win every argument. Just share the Word of God and let Him work on hearts. That is His job anyway. Ours is to treasure His commandments in our own hearts and be ready to give an answer for the hope that lies within us (I Peter 3:15). Be in the Word every day. Memorize it, cherish it, and make it such an integral part of your mind that you can quote it with ease in times of distress and use it to comfort others who may be suffering or confused. It is a mighty, offensive weapon against Satan's power. Our fight is not just defense.

4. Pray

> *Praying always with all prayer and supplication in the Spirit, and watching thereunto with all perseverance and supplication for all saints.*
>
> —*Ephesians 6:18*

After donning the armor of God, we are commanded to pray *always* with *all* prayer. That is a lot of praying. Prayer is essential to the Christian walk. In fact, we are to pray without ceasing (I Thessalonians 5:17). Individually and corporately, we are to approach our heavenly Father with supplication, asking Him for grace and strength to withstand temptation, and with adoration for His glory and love.

Fight the Good Fight: Pray for Our Mediator to Help Us

Most churches talk about prayer more than they actually pray.[55] However, Paul links prayer closely to spiritual warfare in Ephesians 6:18. Prayer is a not only a weapon of spiritual warfare, *prayer is warfare itself.* Praying is warring. It is allying ourselves with God, thus declaring our stance against Satan. The utterance, "Lead us not into temptation, but deliver us from evil" (Matthew 6:13), is taking our battle with the devil to God Himself.

And when we pray to our precious Savior—our Mediator to a holy God—we are praying to One who has

---

55 Lawless, 156.

suffered every temptation we are subjected to. "For we have not an high priest which cannot be touched with the feeling of our infirmities; but was in all points tempted like as we are, yet without sin" (Hebrews 4:15). We are praying to One who understands, who sympathizes, and who does not wish us to succumb to Satan's snares. We pray to One who despises the devil with a divine hatred, who has defeated him in every way, and who desires to help us overcome him in our daily lives.

We pray to One who has overcome the world.

"These things I have spoken unto you," Christ says, "that in me ye might have peace. In the world ye shall have tribulation: but be of good cheer; I have overcome the world" (John 16:33). Oh, these words are thrilling! Our Savior is a mighty warrior, and He has overcome the world, every last bit.

We Do Not Fight Alone

Furthermore, we are not the only ones praying for ourselves. Incredibly, we can be assured that our Mediator—the Son of God Himself—prays for us (John 17; Romans 8:34; Hebrews 7:25).

That is not all. The Holy Spirit also groans on our behalf: "Likewise the Spirit also helpeth our infirmities: for we know not what we should pray for as we ought: but the Spirit itself maketh intercession for us with groanings which cannot be uttered" (Romans 8:26). Not only does the Holy Spirit pray for us, but He also goes beyond the restrictions of our finite language. He transcends the limited abilities of mere words in His passionate, heartfelt intercessions for us.

How humbled we are, how fortunate, how blessed, that the Father not only promises to hear our prayers (Psalm 22:24; 28:6; 34:17), but He is also petitioned by Jesus Christ and the Spirit on our behalf.

5. Position Yourself Firmly

Take your stand, withstand, stand firm.

—Ephesians 6:13, 14

Only after putting on the armor of God are we ready to stand firm.

One piece of advice often given to would-be writers throughout the years is to mix up the verbs and not repeat the same one(s) over and over again—avoid repetitiveness.

Yet, the Apostle Paul doesn't seem to have ever heard this advice in our Ephesians 6 passage, for he repeats the same thing several times just within a sentence or two. He tells us to stand, stand, and stand (vss. 11, 13, 14).

Armies of old formed lines of battle, straight rows of men with shields. These shield-walls of bodies stood rank upon rank. Ancient combat often involved pushing the front line forward against the enemy's until they gave ground. Yes, there was still a great amount of stabbing over and under the shields (and between if the men allowed a space), but there was primarily pushing for dominance at first. Many ancient battles resembled pushing matches of thousands of men until some sort of advantage was gained.

Notice that the command to stand is more than that: it is to stand *firm*. Thus, the command to stand is not merely a command to passively wait and do nothing. Standing does not mean lingering or being at ease. It means to dig in our heels! It means to bend our knees and flex our thighs, though they burn with effort, and strain against the enemy's weight of phalanxes or legions. We must brace ourselves lest we topple. Indeed, this "standing" is an active effort.

If one were to fall down and not stand, this would not only open him up to be stabbed or trampled, but it would also put his brothers at danger. One man falling would make his fellow soldiers to the right and left completely vulnerable. His shield would no longer guard his flanks. Thus, standing firm was (and is) essential, not only for our own safety, but also for the safety of our fellow Christians. It is not only ourselves we hurt, but also others when we fail to stand. So stand as men. Be firm. Push and strain against the devil's hordes.

Conclusion

The Bad News

Satan is a powerful foe who will stop at nothing to hurt God's plans and His people. He is personal, powerful, deceitful, and evil, and his attacks upon us are real and executed with bloodthirsty vengeance. He can cause disease, hinder plans, and incite us to sin.

The Good News

Thank God that, though frightening, Satan is no match for the Almighty who even uses the devil's cruelest schemes for His own glory and the saints' good. Satan is a mere tool in the hands of the master carpenter. And though the work of God in our lives is often painful, it is for His ultimate glory and our good—that is a sure promise (Romans 8:28).

We are given a full set of armor to battle this foe. We are armed with pure truth, glowing righteousness, the beautiful gospel, stalwart faith, sure salvation, and the sharp, two-edged sword of Scripture.

And above all, glorious in His loving power, we have an awesome Mediator who has overcome the world and defeated the devil once and for all.

A Sincere Message from the Authors

Dear Reader, we pray you are comforted. We pray your heart is encouraged. We pray you can rest in the sovereign power of God and the complete victory of Jesus Christ. Are you amazed by the triumph of our Savior? Are you blown away by the beauty of His gospel?

We pray this is the case. But if it is not, please allow us a few questions. Do you perhaps feel that something is missing? Have you come to the end of this work and instead of being comforted, you are frightened or uneasy? Like maybe you have overlooked something important, or don't have what we are talking about? Do you feel confused or uncomfortable by all of this? Do you feel afraid, lost, or that you are suddenly in the dark instead of the light? Does loving Jesus Christ more than anything sound like foreign talk to you? Have you measured yourself against God's word and found yourself lacking?

Don't fear; the gospel is for everyone. If you have read this far and feel uncomfortable, or that you are missing something—that perhaps your faith could be false—be reassured that this can change. Today you can believe in Jesus Christ. You can know Him as your Savior. You can be rescued. "Behold, *now* is the accepted time; behold, *now* is the day of salvation" (II Corinthians 6:2, emphasis added).

It doesn't matter who you are. It doesn't matter if you've heard the gospel your whole life or you're hearing it for the first time. It doesn't matter if you've just realized you know these things in your mind but they aren't in your heart, or you have never heard anything like this before. It doesn't matter what your background is. All of us are dead in our trespasses before Christ rescues us. Dead is dead no matter where you are or what you've done.

And our Lord *promises* that anyone can be saved if they call on Him. "For *whosoever* shall call upon the Lord *shall be saved*" (Romans 10:13, emphasis added). This is a sure promise, just as sure as the deliverance from Satan, and it is made to *all* who call on the name of Jesus.

All you must do is repent of your sins—turn from them and turn to God by His grace—and believe in Jesus Christ. "*Repent* ye: for the kingdom of heaven is at hand" (Matthew 3:2, emphasis added).

> That if thou shalt *confess with thy mouth* the Lord Jesus, and shalt *believe in thine heart* that God hath raised him from the dead, thou shalt be saved. For with the heart man believeth unto righteousness; and with the mouth confession is made unto salvation. For the scripture saith, *Whosoever believeth on him shall not be ashamed.*
>
> —Romans 10:9-11, emphasis added

Dear friends, we serve a Savior who has overcome the world. He has overcome *every temptation*. He has overcome *the devil*. And He has emerged victorious. He can overcome the sin in your heart. He can rescue you and keep you, sanctifying you until the day He comes again (Philippians 1:6).

Now we must fight the good fight. Until heaven, this is our calling.

Death is swallowed up in victory. O death, where is thy sting? O grave, where is thy victory? The sting of death is sin; and the strength of sin is the law. But thanks be to God, which giveth us the victory through our Lord Jesus Christ. Therefore, my beloved brethren, be ye stedfast, unmovable, always abounding in the work of the Lord, forasmuch as ye know that your labour is not in vain in the Lord.

—*1 Corinthians 15:54-58*

Bibliography

Arnold, Clinton E. Powers of Darkness: Principalities & Powers in Paul's Letters. Downers Grove, Illinois: Intervarsity Press, 1992.

Arters, Rod. Satan's Voice – In the Bible or in Your Head. https://rodarters.wordpress.com/2012/09/04/satans-voice-in-the-bible-or-your-head/.

Augustine. The Enchiridion of Faith, Hope and Love. Translated by Thomas S. Hibbs. Washington, D.C.: Regnery Gateway, 1996.

Boyd, Gregory. God At War: The Bible & Spiritual Conflict. Downer's Grove, Illinois: IVP Academic, 1997.

_____. Is God to Blame?: Moving Beyond Pat Answers to the Problem of Evil. Downer's Grove, Illinois: InterVarsity Press, 2003.

Calvin, John. Institutes of the Christian Religion, Volume I. translated by Henry Beveridge. Edinburgh: Calvin Translation Society, 1854; reprint Grand Rapids: Eerdman's, 1958.

Caryl, Joseph. Exposition of Job. Lafayette, Indiana: Sovereign Grace Publishers, 1959.

Ellison, H.L. From Tragedy to Triumph. Carlisle, Pennsylvania: The Paternoster Press, 1958.

Giesler, Norman L. Philosophy of Religion. Eugene, Oregon: Wipf & Stock Publishers, 2003.

Gurnall, William. The Christian in Complete Armour: Or, A Treatise on the Saints' War with the devil. London: William Tegg, 1862.

Haley, John W. Alleged Discrepancies of the Bible. Grand
    Rapids, Michigan: Baker Book House, 1977.

Hartley, John E. The Book of Job. Grand Rapids: Eerdmans
    Publishing, 1988.

Lawless, Chuck. Discipled Warriors: Growing Healthy
    Churches That Are Equipped For Spiritual Warfare.
    Grand Rapids, Michigan: Kregel Publications, 2002.

Leahy, Frederick. Satan Cast Out: A Study in Biblical
    Demonology. Carlisle, Pennsylvania: Banner of Truth
    Trust, 2004.

MacArthur, John. "The Character of Satan." Sermon. Grace
    Community Church, Panorama City, CA, 2000.

Piper, John. God Is the Gospel: Meditations on God's Love as
    the Gift of Himself. Wheaton, Illinois: Crossway Books,
    2005.

_____. "The Sifting of Simon Peter (Luke 22;31-34)."
    Sermon. Bethlehem Baptist Church, Minneapolis,
    Minnesota, April 26, 1981.

Spurgeon, Charles. "Satan Considering the Saints."
    Metropolitan Tabernacle Pulpit, volume 11, pages 193-
    205. Pilgrim Press, 1989.

_____. "Satan A Defeated Foe." page 16. Springdale, PA:
    Whitaker House, 1983.

Turretin, Francis. "On The Necessity of the Atonement."
    Translated by James R. Wilson, in Wilson, James R.
    A Historical Sketch of Opinions on the Atonement.
    Philadelphia, Pennsylvania: James Earle, 1817.

Washer, Paul. "Dating, Courtship, and Marriage," sermon,
    http://bringingtruth.com/OtherStuff/PaulWasherQuotes.
    aspx.

About the Authors

Trevor Johnson,
Missionary and Author

Trevor and Teresa have been married for 17 years. They serve and love a remote tribal group in Papua, Indonesia.

They are both registered nurses and Trevor is an ordained Christian minister. They are deeply aware that all they have and are is by the grace of God, and that any blessings they receive are to be used to bless others. They mean to live their lives in gratitude to a Savior who loves them and gave Himself for them. Confronted by the pains and evils of the world, they desire not to shrink back or shield their eyes, but instead to face the hurts and struggles of others, being like Christ to those who need His love despite their own shortcomings, and to bless others on their journey through life.

Trevor and Teresa have four wonderful children (Noah, 12; Alethea, 9; Perpetua, 5; and Baby Gideon) and two more waiting for them in heaven. They pray their children will grow up as gentle, loving souls who will work for a better world and not merely live for their own comfort and ease.

Trevor and Teresa believe in a sovereign God who weaves all of our lives together for His greater glory.

"Resolved, to live with all my might, while I do live."

~ Jonathan Edwards' Resolutions

"I sought the Lord, and afterward I knew he moved my soul to seek him, seeking me; it was not I that found, O Savior true; no, I was found of thee.

Thou didst reach forth thy hand and mine enfold; I walked and sank not on the storm-vexed sea; 'twas not so much that I on thee took hold, as thou, dear Lord, on me.

I find, I walk, I love, but oh, the whole of love is but my answer, Lord, to thee; for thou wert long beforehand with my soul, always thou lovedst me."

~ Anonymous

Grace Rankin,
Author and Editor

Grace is a Christian author, freelance writer, and editor serving the Lord in Indiana.

She earned her Bachelor's Degree in English from Thomas Edison State University, and uses her love of writing to help others and be a light for Christ.

Grace enjoys writing for Sovereign Grace Missionary Press and offering freelance services through her business, Writing Life. She authored *The Gospel in 5*, a short guidebook on sharing the gospel, and is preparing several novels for publication.

She lives in Indiana with her family and enjoys playing the piano, hiking, reading, and writing fiction.

Because of Christ,

"The blind receive sight and the lame walk, the lepers are cleansed and the deaf hear, the dead are raised up, and the poor have the gospel preached to them."

~ Matthew 11:5 ~

"Come to Me, all who are weary and heavy-laden, and I will give you rest. Take My yoke upon you and learn from Me, for I am gentle and humble in heart, and you will find rest for your souls."

~ Matthew 11:28-29 ~

Fight
THE
good
Fight

Made in the USA
Las Vegas, NV
11 September 2021